The Merrybegot

Contents

OXFORD
UNIVERSITY PRESS

Great Clarendon Street, Oxford OX2 6DP

Oxford University Press is a department of the University of Oxford.
It furthers the University's objective of excellence in research, scholarship,
and education by publishing worldwide in

Oxford   New York

Auckland   Cape Town   Dar es Salaam   Hong Kong   Karachi
Kuala Lumpur   Madrid   Melbourne   Mexico City   Nairobi
New Delhi   Shanghai   Taipei   Toronto

With offices in

Argentina   Austria   Brazil   Chile   Czech Republic   France   Greece
Guatemala   Hungary   Italy   Japan   South Korea   Poland   Portugal
Singapore   Switzerland   Thailand   Turkey   Ukraine   Vietnam

Oxford is a registered trade mark of Oxford University Press
in the UK and in certain other countries

British Library Cataloguing in Publication Data

Data available

ISBN-13: 978-0-19-832647-2
ISBN-10: 0-19-832647-5

10 9 8 7 6 5 4 3 2 1

Printed in Malaysia by Imago.

Acknowledgements

P6l P Gapper/World Religions Photo Library/|Alamy; **p6r** Mike
Greenslade/Alamy; **p7** Bettmann/Corbis.

Illustrations are by Martin Cottam

We are grateful for permission to reprint the following copyright
material in this guide:

Miriam Bay: review of *The Merrybegot*, reprinted by permission of the
author and the Devon Library and Information Services.

James Berardinelli: review of the film 'The Crucible' from
www.reelviews.net website, used with permission of the author.

Frederic Brussat: review of the film 'The Crucible', copyright ©
Frederic and Mary Brussat, from www.SprituAlityandPractice.com
website, used by permission of the author.

Adele Geras: extract from 'Piskies and Puritans: *The Merrybegot* by Julie
Hearn', *The Guardian*, 12.2.05, copyright © Guardian Newspapers Ltd
2005, reprinted by permission of Guardian Newspapers Ltd.

Julie Hearn: letter used by permission of the author.

We have tried to trace and contact all copyright holders before
publication. If notified, the publisher will be pleased to rectify any
errors or omissions at the earliest opportunity.

Key to icons:

 Pair or group activity

 A resources sheet from the Teacher's
Pack supports this activity.

The Merrybegot

A Letter from Julie Hearn

Dear Reader,

I got the idea for *The Merrybegot* while studying witchcraft at Oxford University. No, I wasn't taught, as Nell is, how to soothe a truculent pig or make a lad swoon with desire, but I did learn a lot of fascinating — and very scary — facts about the prejudices, religious strife and social tensions that sent so many people to the gallows, as witches, during the English Civil War.

And I found myself wondering: what must it have been like, living in such turbulent times? As an old woman, perhaps — a village healer, grown so muddled with age that she is making dangerous mistakes? Or a young girl too outspoken and independent for her own good? Or a pregnant teenager terrified by the changes to her body and desperate to keep them hidden? All three of these characters found their way to an imaginary village in the west of England, and *The Merrybegot* began…

It took me almost a year and a half to write this novel, but a good six months of that time was spent in libraries researching everything from West Country folklore to old herbal remedies. I have a ritual, before I start a new novel, of going shopping for a special notebook in which to jot down all the bits of information I think might be useful. *The Merrybegot* notebook has a picture on the front of an angel holding a glass vase — it is dreamy and old-fashioned!

I write straight onto a computer, in an office in my garden. It's a small space, my office, but very peaceful. The walls and ceiling are painted bright pink and green, which are my favourite colours, and the books I read as a child are on a shelf above the window. When I write I see and hear everything that happens, like a film in my head, and my characters are as real to me as living, breathing people.

Although *The Merrybegot* is historical fantasy, the issues I tackle — unwanted pregnancy, abortion, religious intolerance and euthanasia, to name just a few — are as important today as they ever were. So I hope the book gives you plenty to think about. Most of all, though, I hope you enjoy it.

Julie Hearn

Julie Hearn
www.julie-hearn.com

Never Judge a Book by its Cover

Never Judge

Wise words

There may be truth in this wise saying, but many readers say that the cover is often an important factor in choosing and buying a book.

What can you tell?

Here are two of the covers that have been used for *The Merrybegot*.

- ◉ Which would make you pick the book up, and why?
- ◉ How do feel about having a photograph on the cover? Does this affect the way you interact with the book?
- ◉ What features do you think are important when designing a cover?

The Merrybegot

Predicting what will follow

- Test out whether you can judge a book by its cover by making one prediction from each cover about what *The Merrybegot* will be about.
- Compare these in small groups. Are there similarities in your predictions?
- Keep a note of your predictions so that you can return to them later.

Will your predictions come true?

May Day – Innocent Fun or Heathen Frolicking?

Celebrating May Day

Even to the present day, many people celebrate the pagan customs of May Day. In some English villages, the coming of May is celebrated by the crowning of a May Queen and by dancing around the maypole, just as it has been for centuries. Long ago, many people would wake up at first light and go out to find flowers and branches to decorate their homes. Women would put flowers in their hair, which is why most May Queens today have a coronet of flowers.

Ancient Festival of Beltane

Celebrated on the night of 30 April and into 1 May, Beltane is a fire festival that heralds the coming of summer and the fertility of the coming year. Beltane is a Celtic word that means 'fires of Bel' (a Celtic god).

The biggest Beltane celebrations take place in Edinburgh, where a torchlit procession ends with the 'marriage' of the May Queen and the Green Man on Carlton Hill.

Wild water is supposed to have magic qualities on May morning, and people used to wash in dew to make themselves beautiful, or drink water from streams or springs to bring good health.

> *Why did people gather branches on May morning?*

> *Why were cattle walked through the embers of a fire?*

You Decide...

See what else you can find out about May Day celebrations. Then prepare a presentation on whether you think they are innocent fun.

- Use images and facts from this page and from books and websites you can find.
- Decide on the most exciting way of sharing your findings. You may want to make a word and picture collage, a dance, or formally present the evidence that helped you reach your decision.

The Merrybegot

Piskies and Fairies? What's That All About?

Marketing piskies

Piskies and fairies are important characters in the plot of *The Merrybegot*. But where do they come from? And do they have a place in teenage fiction, or are they just the stuff of bedtime stories for younger children?

Playing the Text Detective

Read the following fact box and decide whether Julie Hearn's little people match any of these characteristics.

> ### Fact or legend?
>
> - Piskies date back to when the south west of England was known as Kerniu, an area covering what is now Cornwall, Devon and Somerset.
> - Piskies look like old men with wrinkled faces; they are small with red hair. They dress in the colours of the earth, especially green, using grass and moss for their materials.
> - Piskies are the sworn enemies of fairies.
> - Piskies are cheerful, with a prankish nature. They help the elderly or infirm, but are likely to lead able-bodied travellers astray on the moor.

Fairy folklore

There have been many supposed sightings of fairies. A site in Sussex is supposed to be the last place in England inhabited by fairies before they disappeared for good.

If you have seen *A Midsummer Night's Dream* by William Skakespeare, you will remember the fairy king and queen Oberon and Titania, and the mischievous Puck. 'Puck' or 'Pook' comes from the Saxon word 'Puca', which means a goblin.

Many stories about fairies seem to contain a lesson or moral. From your own childhood you may remember stories about the tooth fairy, who brings money for milk teeth if you clean your teeth well.

What role do the fairies play?

'The fairies in *The Merrybegot* are helpful in two really important ways, but they are also cold-hearted and selfish creatures.'

- Decide whether you agree with this view. As you read the book, collect evidence of the way the fairies behave and how they affect events.

Drawing on the evidence

- Find a way of showing the main characteristics of the piskies and the fairies on a flow chart or spider diagram.
- Add the key ways in which they affect the plot to this diagram.

The Merrybegot

Telling the Tale
with Two Voices

Choosing the storyteller

One of the most important decisions a writer has to make is *who* is going to tell the story. Julie Hearn chooses to use two voices to give the reader two views of events in *The Merrybegot*. This is called *alternate narrative form*.

Exploring the two voices

Most of the story is told by a narrator in the present tense, with detailed and lively descriptions and characters showing their personalities by the things they say and do:

> It is seconds which count now. Real seconds. Human seconds.
>   'Cut the cord!' squeals the consort – beside the moss now and jumping up and down in a frenzy. 'Cut the cord, you great booby!'
> (page 63)

Some of the story is told by Patience, the minister's daughter, in the past tense and in the first person. It is dated over 40 years later. Patience is making a confession in her older years, looking back on the events.

> 'I never meant it to end the way it did. Grace might have done, but not me. Grace was fifteen, as artful as a snake, and already on the slippery slope to Hell.' (page 1)

- ◉ Why might Patience be making this confession, and what might the outcome be?
- ◉ Can you think of any reason why it might be to her advantage to be vague or seem ignorant of certain events?

Revealing character

Patience reveals her own character by the things she says and does, whereas Nell is described by the narrator, other characters and her own actions.

- ◉ Based on the evidence on the next page, who would you most like to meet? Patience or Nell?
- ◉ How would you describe each character in three words?

The Merrybegot

Tale with Two Voices

[Patience:]
'She started it'
'It was her fault'
'I'm scared'
'We went too far'
'You're vain'
'She's a sinner. Serves her right.'
'I felt compelled to do her bidding'

[Narrator:]
'Nell is young and wild, but the gift of healing is in her'
'My granddaughter is here to learn'
Nell returns his gaze with as much courage as she can muster
The cunning woman's granddaughter is chasing a pig
Her stomach rumbles beneath her pinafore, but she is used to that
There are things Nell ought to be doing, but she stays where she is

investigating why

As you read on, think about why Julie Hearn chooses to use the alternate narrative structure to tell her story.

- ◉ Is it to give a complete account of events?
- ◉ Are both accounts truthful?
- ◉ Do bias and opinion play a part in one or both narratives?
- ◉ Which voice do you find most convincing, and why?
- ◉ What is the advantage of each type of narration?
- ◉ Does one voice reveal more about a character or events than the other?

Who has the more truthful voice, m'dear?

The Merrybegot

Granny Answers Your Questions...

Who's writing in?

Read each of these letters and decide which character has written each one.

Cold-hearted sweetheart

On May Day, my boyfriend and I were taking part in the usual celebrations in the woods. We were having such fun and were really happy. He seemed to be in love with me and kept telling me how pretty I am. I trusted him completely.

Recently I have discovered that our frolicking is to become obvious to everyone. When I told him of our 'news' he looked really shocked and didn't even comfort me. I had to ask him to stand by me and marry me. He told me he needs to join the soldiers, but will come back for me. I am not sure whether I believe him. Was I wrong to trust him? Do you think he will come back for me and our baby? What should I do?

Granny replies...

It is important that you stay calm. You're probably feeling humiliated and let down at this time; you will have the child to look after and the comments of people to bear. Your boyfriend will go off to join the soldiers without a care in the world. 'Twas ever thus. Men and boys get away with all kinds. Take heart that the child will be very special... 'twill be a Merrybegot!

Life or death decision

I recently delivered a baby for a fairy couple and in payment they gave me the caul, which is a kind of magic bandage that will save a human life. The only trouble is that it can be used only once. I want to use it to save my Granny, who is very old and losing her mind, but she says her time has come. Should I use it to save her anyway, or save the caul in case I need it myself? There is also a sickly baby, and who knows what might happen in the future? I am so confused. It is awful having the power of life and death. Please give me some advice.

Reading pages 156 to 161 will help you decide what advice Granny might give.

The Merrybegot

Confused

I am worried about my sister. She has been acting very strangely recently. She began by sneaking out at night when she thought I was asleep. Another time she forced me to go with her to look in a trunk that had belonged to our late mother. She was looking in a looking glass, which is very sinful. Worst of all, I took a lovely little emerald frog with ruby eyes and kept it. Now she is refusing to let us get up; we have to stay in bed and she makes me pretend that I am taken over by evil spirits. It is all her fault and I don't know what to do.

> Reading Patience's confessions (up to page 108) will give you more to think about. What might Granny advise?

Write to reply

Decide how Granny would reply to 'Confused' and write a short letter of 100 words that:

⊙ gives useful advice to the letter writer

⊙ uses your knowledge of the characters involved

⊙ includes the kinds of words and phrases that Granny might use.

The Merrybegot

Freeze That Frame!

The final journey?

The Merrybegot

Bringing the storyboard to life!

The storyboard will help your group create a dramatic freeze frame.

⦿ One of you should become the sculptor and position your fellow group members as 'models' to recreate the storyboard and show the relationships between characters.

⦿ The body language of each character should show the emotions they are feeling.

⦿ Place another student behind each character who has a thought bubble in the storyboard. This student will say what the character is thinking or feeling.

Use the character list below to help you.

Each freeze frame scene could be brought to life in sequence, to try to really understand what the characters might be feeling and how their thoughts change as the scene goes on.

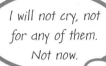

I will not cry, not for any of them. Not now.

Nell

Minister Madden

My eyes are deceiving me. I can hardly breathe. She looks exactly like... No words will leave my mouth!

Witchfinder General

I am not doing this just for the twenty shillings. These ignorant fools need to know what will happen if they do not conform.

Mistress Bramlow

I must help the poor innocent child – she has no one else.

Hangman

What the devil is going on? Who is this soldier? I am sure I have seen him somewhere.

Soldier

This Matthew Hopkins is an evil hypocrite. He is sentencing an innocent child to death, just because she can heal people, but mostly so he can line his pocket! Is this God's love?

The Merrybegot

Review Time

What's in a review?

A review can help you decide whether to watch a film or read a particular book. If you are interested in 'witch hunts' or bullying, then the reviews on these pages are for you!

The theme of 'witch hunts' has been explored by many authors. Arthur Miller wrote a play called *The Crucible* in which a group of young girls claim to be possessed by demons in order to get their own way or to get out of trouble. This has been performed in theatres all over the world and there are several film versions.

Movie Review

by Frederic Brussat

The Crucible

Nicholas Hytner 20th Century Fox Home Entertainment 11/96 VHS

In 1692, a band of young girls from the Puritan community of Salem go into the woods at night for some forbidden revelry. After they are seen by the town's conservative minister, two of their number fall into a mysterious sleep. Another clergyman who specializes in witchcraft is summoned to Salem. He draws out a confession from a frightened maid that she has made a pact with the devil. Soon the other girls are accusing certain members of the community of being agents of Lucifer. Salem is torn apart by paranoia and hatred.

As one of the most sobering and prophetic films of 1996, The Crucible compels us to recognize the shadow side of our lives, including the evil inside us. The ending also compels us to think about whether there is anything that we would be willing to die for.

The Crucible (1996)

A Film Review by James Berardinelli

The film opens with a seemingly harmless event – Abigail Williams (Winona Ryder), Mary Warren (Karron Graves), Mercy Lewis (Kali Rocha), and several other Salem village girls attend a secret voodoo ritual in the woods.

However, when the local preacher, Reverend Parris (Bruce Davison), stumbles upon the proceedings, and two of the girls subsequently fall into coma-like states, witchcraft is suspected, and an expert in the field, Reverend Hale (Rob Campbell), is brought in to investigate.

The Merrybegot

There are many books where a woman is persecuted on the pretence that the community is being saved from evil. *The Merrybegot* is an excellent example. See what these readers thought of it…

An extract from Adele Geras' review for *The Guardian*:

Julie Hearn has written an absorbing story in which several plot strands wind over and under one another like ribbons on a maypole to create an intricately braided narrative.

The story is set in the seventeenth century. It begins with a confession written in 1692, by the simple-minded younger daughter of the man who was minister in Nell's village more than 40 years before. We then move to 1645, and a story written in the present tense mainly from Nell's point of view. The life of the village, its customs, inhabitants and especially the conflict between the old religion of paganism and a puritan Christianity is wonderfully evoked.

The text is peppered with actual spells… We learn what happens to Nell, her grandmother and the minister's two daughters. The plot is dramatic and eventful and takes in Nell's visit to the land of the fairies to deliver a child.

Some of the things we are asked to believe are fantastical, but the author presents her supernatural effects in such a matter-of-fact way that they seem only an extension of the wonders to be found in nature all around us.

And this review contributed to a website by a young reader:

Wow! What can I say? This book is truly amazing. Julie Hearn's original and wild style of writing reinforces the story and make the main characters that much more three-dimensional and believable. If you were intrigued by Arthur Miller's *The Crucible* and hooked by *Witch Child* by Celia Rees, then this is the book to read. It's amazing! I would give this book 9 out of 10.

Comparing Texts

From reading these reviews and perhaps watching a clip from the film, what similarities have you noticed between *The Crucible* and *The Merrybegot*?

Your own web review

Try writing your own 70-word review for a website aimed at your age group.

⊙ Mention interesting parts of the plot or characters to grab the reader's interest.

⊙ Include a comment on Julie Hearn's style.

⊙ Add your score out of 10.

Pathways... to Another Good Read

Thematically linked texts

The Crucible by Arthur Miller

ISBN 0-4137-0980-9

You have already heard something about *The Crucible* by Arthur Miller on pages 14–15. Try to watch the video, or read the playscript.

Witch Child by Celia Rees

ISBN 0-7475-5009-3

Celia Rees, mentioned in one of the reviews on page 15, also writes an intriguing story on the same themes, so look out for *Witch Child*. This book, written in diary form, is also set in seventeenth-century England and features Mary and her grandmother, who is actually hanged as a witch! Mary flees to America, helped by a mysterious noblewoman. Do you see any similarities?

Sorceress by Celia Rees

ISBN 0-7475-5568-0

You might also want to try *Sorceress* by Celia Rees – the sequel to Witch Child.

The Burning Time by Carol Matas

ISBN 0-4402-1978-7

A young girl's mother, the local healer and midwife, is arrested for witchcraft.

Complementary non-fiction

If you want to give your brain a real work-out you could do some investigations into the so-called 'witch hunts' that took place in the twentieth century, where different groups of people were persecuted. A famous example is McCarthyism, where US Senator Joseph McCarthy rooted out people he felt were communists. It was this that gave Arthur Miller his motivation for writing *The Crucible*. Here are a couple of books to start you off on your quest:

Witch-Hunt by Chris Priestley

ISBN 0-3408-6056-1

The chilling true story of the Salem witches.

Witch-Hunt Mysteries of the Salem Witch Trials by Marc Aronson

ISBN 0-6898-4864-1

This carefully researched book is organized by timeline, making it easy to follow. It shows how the smallest details are vital in uncovering truth. A must for budding detectives!

Witchfinders by Malcolm Gaskill

ISBN 0-7195-6120-5

This is the true story of Matthew Hopkins – intended for adults, but loads of interesting facts!

Light relief!

Sabrina the Teenage Witch

ISBN 0-6710-1433-1

If you want a quick read, you could go for the *Sabrina the Teenage Witch* series. At least one of these gives an interpretation of a witch trial. And of course, if you are feeling very lazy, you could just watch the relevant episode of the series on the TV re-runs!

Happy hunting!